ECHOES OF THE PAST

HEALING THROUGH PAST LIFE REGRESSION

DR. MINAKSHI BANSAL

DEDICATION

To all the souls who have walked before me,

To all the souls who walk beside me now,

And to all the souls who will walk after me,

This book is dedicated to the eternal journey of the soul.

ᚦᚦᚦ

Contents

Prayer — *vii*

About The Author — *ix*

Preface — *xiii*

1. Unlock The Secrets Of Your Soul's Journey. — 1

Part 1

2. Heal Old Wounds And Embrace Your True Self. — 7

Part 2

3. Discover The Hidden Patterns Shaping Your Life. — 13

Part 3

4. Uncover The Root Causes Of Your Fears And Anxieties. — 19

Part 4

5. Find Peace And Resolution In Past Life Connections. — 25

Part 5

6. Reframe Challenging Experiences With New Understanding. — 31

Part 6

7. Transform Your Relationships Through Forgiveness And Compassion. — 37

Part 7

8. Awaken To Your Soul's Purpose And Potential. — 43

Part 8

9. Reconnect With Lost Loved Ones And Spirit Guides. — 49

Part 9

10. Gain Clarity On Your Life's Path And Direction. — 55

Part 10

11. Break Free From Limiting Beliefs And Self-sabotage. — 61

Part 11

Contents

12. Release Emotional Baggage And Reclaim Your Power.   67

Part 12

13. Cultivate Inner Peace And Self-love Through Past Life   73

    Healing.

Part 13

14. Embrace The Wisdom And Lessons Of Your Past Lives.   79

Part 14

15. Create A More Fulfilling And Joyful Present.   85

Part 15

16. Experience Profound Healing And Transformation.   91

Part 16

17. Step Into Your Full Potential And Live A Life Of Purpose.   97

Part 17

18. Journey Through Time To Uncover Your Soul's History.   103

Part 18

19. Embark On A Path Of Self-discovery And Healing.   109

Part 19

20. Unleash The Power Of Past Life Regression For Lasting   115

    Change.

Part 20

21. SUMMARY   121

Citation and References   125

Other Books of the Author   127

CONTACT   133

Prayer

"Om Bhadram Karnebhih Shrinuyama Devah

Bhadram Pashyemakshabhiryajatrah

Sthirairangais Tushtuvamsastanubhih

Vyashema Devahitam Yadayuh

Svasti Na Indro Vriddhashravah

Svasti Nah Pusha Vishwavedah

Svasti Nastarkshyo Arishtanemih

Svasti No Brihaspatir Dadhatu

Om Shantih Shantih Shantih"

This mantra is a prayer for universal well-being, invoking the blessings of various deities for protection, health, and happiness. It emphasizes the importance of experiencing the auspicious through all senses and living a life aligned with divine purpose. The repetition of "Shantih" at the end signifies a deep desire for peace in the individual, the environment, and the universe at large. This mantra is often recited as a prayer for peace, prosperity, and the physical and spiritual well-being of all beings.

ᗡᗡᗡ

About The Author

This book represents the culmination of extensive research and meticulous analysis, incorporating a diverse range of sources, including numerous books, scholarly studies, and personal experiences. Additionally, I have scoured various websites to gather relevant information and data essential for the compilation of this work. I have taken every precaution to ensure the accuracy of the information presented and have diligently cited all sources to acknowledge their contributions.

From her earliest days, Minakshi was distinguished by an insatiable appetite for reading. Her literary universe was inhabited by characters and narratives that spanned ethical tales, motivational and inspirational stories, and the mythic parables imbued with life lessons. This voracious reading habit was not merely for personal edification but was driven by a desire to distill and disseminate the essence of these narratives to foster the development of students and peers alike. She was particularly captivated by the lives and teachings of historical figures and spiritual leaders such as Adi Shankaracharya, Swami Vivekananda, Dr. APJ Abdul Kalam, Mahamana Pandit Madan Mohan Malviya, Mahatma Gandhi, Sardar Vallabhai Patel, and Vinoba Bhave, among others. Their philosophies and life stories fueled her ambition to embody their ideals of resilience, selflessness, and relentless pursuit of knowledge.

Dr. Minakshi's academic and practical engagement with psychology has been equally noteworthy. As a research scholar, her focus has been on exploring the intricate tapestry of the human psyche, aiming to unlock the potential for psychological well-being and societal harmony. Her scholarly work is complemented by her active involvement in social work, where she employs her academic insights to make tangible differences in the lives of the underprivileged. Her endeavours in social work are characterized by an innovative approach that combines traditional wisdom with contemporary psychological practices to address the multifaceted challenges faced by these communities.

Her artistic talents, another facet of her diverse capabilities, are not merely a personal passion but also serve as a medium through which she communicates and connects with others. Her art, rich in symbolism and emotional depth, reflects her philosophical inquiries and social concerns, offering viewers a glimpse into the breadth of her intellect and the depth of her compassion.

In addition to her contributions to the arts and social sciences, Dr. Minakshi has embraced the healing arts of Pranic Healing, mastering the techniques developed by Master Choa Kok Sui. This practice, which focuses on the manipulation of Prana or life energy to heal the body and aura, has been both a personal journey of discovery and a means through which she extends her healing touch to others. Her proficiency in Pranic Healing is complemented by her advocacy and teaching of various forms of meditation aimed at rejuvenation, personal betterment, and the cultivation of harmony within individuals and communities alike.

Dr. Minakshi's life is a narrative of relentless pursuit, not just of personal achievement but of the upliftment and empowerment of society at large. Her diverse interests and talents—spanning the arts, literature, psychology, and the healing practices—converge on a singular path of service. She embodies the spirit of the luminaries who inspired her, channelling their legacy through her actions and teachings. Through her books, art, and social initiatives, she continues to inspire a new generation to embark on their own journeys of self-discovery, resilience, and altruism.

Her commitment to social betterment, particularly her focus on uplifting underprivileged children, reflects a deep understanding of the transformative potential of education and personal development. By integrating her knowledge of psychology, her artistic sensibilities, and her healing practices, Dr. Bansal has developed a holistic approach to social work that addresses both the immediate needs and the long-term well-being of the communities she serves.

As an author, Dr. Minakshi's writings offer a blend of inspirational insights, practical wisdom, and reflective contemplations drawn from her extensive reading and life experiences. Her books serve as a guide for those seeking to navigate the complexities of life with grace, resilience, and purpose. Through her narratives, she extends an invitation to her readers to explore the depths of their own potential and to contribute meaningfully to the collective well-being of society.

In Dr. Minakshi Bansal, we find a remarkable synthesis of the artist, the scholar, the healer, and the social activist. Her life's work stands as a beacon of hope and a source of inspiration for individuals seeking to make a difference in the world. Her story is a compelling reminder of the power of individual action, rooted in compassion and driven by a profound commitment to the betterment of humanity. Dr. Minakshi's legacy is not just in the tangible outcomes of her efforts but in the enduring spirit of inquiry, empathy, and service that she embodies.

Preface

In the quiet corners of our minds, whispers of forgotten lives echo through the corridors of time. We are not merely the sum of our present experiences, but rather a mosaic of countless lives lived, lessons learned, and loves lost. This book is an invitation to embark on a journey of self-discovery, to delve into the depths of your soul's history, and to uncover the hidden patterns that have shaped your present reality.

Through the transformative power of past life regression, you will have the opportunity to explore the uncharted territories of your subconscious, to reconnect with lost loved ones, to understand the root causes of your fears and anxieties, and to embrace the wisdom and lessons of your past lives. This is a journey of healing, of understanding, and of reclaiming your power.

In this book, I will share with you the knowledge and insights I have gained through years of studying and practicing past life regression. I will guide you through the process of accessing your past lives, interpreting the information that emerges, and integrating the lessons you learn into your present life. This is not a book for the faint of heart. It is a journey that requires courage, vulnerability, and a willingness to confront the shadows of your past. But it is also a journey of profound healing and transformation, a journey that can lead you to a deeper understanding of yourself and your purpose in life.

As you delve into the pages of this book, you will be invited to explore the many facets of past life regression. You will learn how to identify and heal old wounds, release emotional baggage, and break free from self-limiting beliefs. You will discover how to reframe challenging experiences with new understanding, transform your relationships through forgiveness and compassion, and awaken to your soul's purpose and potential.

You will also have the opportunity to reconnect with lost loved ones and spirit guides, gain clarity on your life's path and direction, and cultivate inner peace and self-love. This book is a guide, a companion, and a source of inspiration as you embark on your own journey of self-discovery and healing.

The path of past life regression is not always easy. It can be an emotional journey, as you confront the shadows of your past and release the pain and suffering that you have carried with you for lifetimes. But it is also a journey of profound healing and transformation, a journey that can lead you to a deeper understanding of yourself and your purpose in life.

It is my hope that this book will empower you to embrace the wisdom and lessons of your past lives, to heal old wounds, and to step into your full potential. It is my hope that it will inspire you to live a more authentic, joyful, and fulfilling life, aligned with your soul's deepest desires.

Dr. Minakshi Bansal
Social Activist
Ahmedabad, Gujarat, Bharat

ᖷᖷᖷ

ONE

UNLOCK THE SECRETS OF YOUR SOUL'S JOURNEY.

In the tapestry of existence, the threads of our lives intertwine, weaving a complex and beautiful pattern that extends far beyond our current understanding. We are not merely isolated individuals, but rather, eternal beings on a timeless journey of growth, learning, and self-discovery. This journey transcends the boundaries of a single lifetime, carrying the echoes of past experiences, relationships, and lessons that shape who we are today. Past life regression offers a powerful tool to unravel the mysteries of our soul's voyage, providing profound insights into the hidden patterns and influences that have shaped our lives.

By delving into the depths of our subconscious mind, we can access the vast reservoir of memories and emotions that lie dormant within us. Through hypnosis or guided meditation, we can embark on a journey back in time, revisiting past lives and reconnecting with forgotten aspects of ourselves. These experiences can be incredibly vivid and transformative, offering a unique perspective on our current challenges, fears, and desires.

The concept of reincarnation, or the belief in the rebirth of the soul into different bodies, is central to the practice of past life regression. While not everyone may subscribe to this belief system, the therapeutic benefits of exploring past lives are undeniable. Even if viewed as metaphorical or symbolic representations of our subconscious mind, past life regression can provide valuable insights into our deepest motivations, beliefs, and behaviors.

One of the most profound benefits of past life regression is the ability to identify and heal old wounds and traumas. By revisiting past experiences, we can gain a deeper understanding of the root causes of our current emotional and physical struggles. We may discover unresolved conflicts, unprocessed grief, or deeply ingrained patterns of self-sabotage that have been carried over from previous lifetimes. By facing these issues head-on, we can release pent-up emotions, forgive ourselves and others, and ultimately break free from the cycle of pain and suffering.

Past life regression can also help us to gain a greater understanding of our relationships with others. We may discover karmic connections with loved ones, soulmates, or even adversaries, shedding light on the dynamics of our current interactions. By recognizing the karmic patterns that play out in our relationships, we can learn valuable lessons about forgiveness, compassion, and unconditional love.

Another significant benefit of past life regression is the opportunity to reconnect with our soul's purpose and potential. By exploring our past lives, we may discover hidden talents, skills, or passions that have been carried over from previous incarnations. We may also gain a clearer understanding of our life's mission and the unique gifts we have to offer the world. This newfound clarity can empower us to make bold choices, pursue our dreams, and live a more authentic and fulfilling life.

Past life regression can also offer a sense of closure and resolution for unresolved issues from the past. By revisiting past lives, we may be able to say goodbye to loved ones, make amends for past mistakes, or simply gain a sense of peace and acceptance about difficult experiences. This can be particularly helpful for those who have experienced loss, trauma, or unresolved grief.

While the benefits of past life regression are numerous, it is important to approach this practice with an open mind and a healthy dose of skepticism. Not all experiences may be accurate or meaningful, and it is important to trust your intuition and discernment when interpreting the information that emerges. It is also crucial to work with a qualified and experienced practitioner who can guide you through the process safely and effectively.

In conclusion, past life regression offers a unique and powerful way to unlock the secrets of your soul's journey. By delving into the depths of your subconscious mind, you can gain profound insights into your past, present, and future. Whether you believe in reincarnation or not, the therapeutic benefits of exploring past lives are undeniable. By healing old wounds, gaining clarity on your life's purpose, and reconnecting with your soul's potential, you can embark on a transformative journey of self-discovery and healing.

ppp

In the echoes of the past, we find the keys to our present. Our soul's journey is a tapestry woven through time, and within its threads lie the answers we seek for healing and growth. By embracing the wisdom of our past lives, we unlock the door to our true potential.

TWO

HEAL OLD WOUNDS AND EMBRACE YOUR TRUE SELF.

In the labyrinthine depths of our being, we carry the weight of old wounds, traumas, and unresolved emotions that shape our present reality. These hidden scars, often buried deep within our subconscious, can manifest as anxieties, fears, limiting beliefs, and self-destructive patterns. Past life regression offers a unique pathway to confront and heal these wounds, allowing us to break free from the shackles of the past and embrace our true selves.

Through the lens of past life regression, we recognize that our current experiences are not isolated incidents but rather echoes of previous lifetimes. The unresolved traumas and emotional baggage we carry from past lives can significantly impact our present well-being, hindering our personal growth and potential. By delving into these past experiences, we can gain profound insights into the origins of our pain, allowing us to address and heal the root causes.

One of the most common ways in which past life regression facilitates healing is by identifying and releasing trapped emotions.

When we experience traumatic events, the associated emotions can become trapped in our energy field, creating blockages that manifest as physical or emotional ailments. By revisiting these past experiences, we can allow these emotions to surface and be processed, releasing the energetic hold they have on us.

Past life regression also helps us to reframe challenging experiences with a new perspective. Often, we carry distorted or negative interpretations of past events, which can lead to feelings of guilt, shame, or resentment. By revisiting these events through the lens of past life regression, we can gain a more objective understanding of the situation, recognizing the lessons learned and the growth that resulted from the experience. This shift in perspective can be incredibly liberating, allowing us to forgive ourselves and others and move forward with a renewed sense of compassion and understanding.

Another powerful aspect of past life regression is the ability to identify and release karmic patterns. Karma, the law of cause and effect, suggests that our actions in past lives can create energetic debts or imbalances that carry over into our present incarnation. By recognizing these patterns, we can consciously choose to break free from them, making amends for past mistakes and creating a more positive trajectory for our lives.

Through past life regression, we can also reconnect with our soul's wisdom and inner guidance. By tapping into the vast knowledge and experience we have accumulated over countless lifetimes, we can gain valuable insights into our current challenges and opportunities. This connection to our higher self can provide us with a sense of clarity, purpose, and direction, allowing us to make choices that are aligned with our true values and aspirations.

The process of healing old wounds and embracing our true selves through past life regression is not always easy. It requires courage, vulnerability, and a willingness to face the depths of our being. However, the rewards are immeasurable. By releasing the burdens of the past, we can create space for joy, abundance, and authentic expression.

As we heal our old wounds, we begin to peel back the layers of conditioning and societal expectations that have obscured our true nature. We discover our unique gifts, talents, and passions, and we find the courage to express them fully in the world. We learn to love and accept ourselves unconditionally, embracing our imperfections as part of our human experience.

In the tapestry of our lives, each thread represents a unique experience, a lesson learned, a challenge overcome. By weaving together the threads of our past, present, and future, we create a beautiful and intricate design that reflects the depth and complexity of our being. Past life regression allows us to explore this tapestry, unraveling the knots and tangles that have held us back, and revealing the true beauty and brilliance that lies within.

In conclusion, healing old wounds and embracing our true selves through past life regression is a transformative journey of self-discovery and empowerment. By confronting our past traumas, releasing trapped emotions, and reconnecting with our soul's wisdom, we can break free from the limitations of our past and step into a future of infinite possibilities. This journey is not always easy, but it is undoubtedly worth it. For in the process of healing our past, we open ourselves up to a life of greater joy, love, and fulfillment.

ᗡᗡᗡ

The scars of yesterday need not define our tomorrow. Through past life regression, we can gently unravel the knots of trauma and pain, allowing the light of healing to illuminate our path towards a more fulfilling and joyful present.

THREE

DISCOVER THE HIDDEN PATTERNS SHAPING YOUR LIFE.

Life often unfolds as a series of seemingly random events, leaving us wondering about the underlying forces that shape our experiences. We may find ourselves repeating the same mistakes, attracting similar types of relationships, or struggling with recurring themes and challenges.

Past life regression offers a unique lens through which we can examine these patterns, uncovering the hidden connections between our past and present lives and gaining profound insights into the underlying causes of our current circumstances.

Through the exploration of past lives, we begin to recognize that our current reality is not a isolated incident but rather a continuation of a larger narrative that spans multiple lifetimes. The choices we made, the relationships we formed, and the lessons we learned in previous incarnations have left indelible imprints on our soul, shaping our beliefs, values, and behaviors in the present. By delving into these past experiences, we can unveil the hidden patterns that have been woven into the fabric of our lives.

One of the most common patterns that emerges through past life regression is the repetition of karmic themes. Karma, the law of cause and effect, suggests that our actions in past lives create energetic debts or imbalances that carry over into our present incarnation.

These karmic patterns can manifest in various ways, such as recurring relationship dynamics, financial struggles, or health issues. By recognizing these patterns, we can consciously choose to break free from them, making amends for past mistakes and creating a more positive trajectory for our lives.

Past life regression can also reveal hidden talents, skills, or passions that have been carried over from previous incarnations. We may discover a natural aptitude for a particular field, a deep-seated desire to help others, or a creative spark that has been dormant for lifetimes. By acknowledging and embracing these innate gifts, we can unlock our full potential and live a more fulfilling and purposeful life.

Another significant pattern that can be uncovered through past life regression is the repetition of soul contracts or agreements. These are agreements that we make with other souls before incarnating, outlining the lessons we wish to learn, the experiences we wish to have, and the relationships we wish to form.

By recognizing these soul contracts, we can gain a deeper understanding of our current relationships and life circumstances, recognizing the purpose and meaning behind our experiences.

Past life regression can also shed light on our fears, phobias, and anxieties. Often, these deep-seated fears are rooted in traumatic experiences from past lives. By revisiting these experiences, we can reframe them with a new perspective, releasing the emotional charge associated with them and freeing ourselves from their grip.

The process of discovering the hidden patterns shaping our lives through past life regression can be both illuminating and challenging. It requires a willingness to confront our past, to acknowledge our own responsibility for our choices and actions, and to embrace the lessons that our experiences have taught us. However, the rewards are immeasurable.

By understanding the underlying causes of our current circumstances, we can make conscious choices to create a more fulfilling and joyful life.

Through past life regression, we can gain a deeper understanding of our soul's journey, recognizing the interconnectedness of our experiences across multiple lifetimes. We can heal old wounds, break free from karmic patterns, and reconnect with our soul's purpose.

This newfound awareness can empower us to live a more authentic and purposeful life, aligned with our deepest values and aspirations.

As we delve into the hidden patterns shaping our lives, we may discover that we are not victims of circumstance but rather co-creators of our own reality. We have the power to choose our thoughts, our beliefs, and our actions, and by doing so, we can shape our destiny.

Past life regression offers a powerful tool for self-discovery and empowerment, allowing us to tap into the wisdom of our soul and create a life that is truly aligned with our highest potential.

In conclusion, discovering the hidden patterns shaping our lives through past life regression is a transformative journey of self-discovery and healing. By exploring our past lives, we can gain profound insights into the underlying causes of our current circumstances, allowing us to break free from limiting beliefs, heal old wounds, and create a more fulfilling and joyful life.

This journey is not always easy, but it is undoubtedly worth it. For in the process of uncovering the hidden patterns of our past, we open ourselves up to a future of infinite possibilities.

ꔇꔇꔇ

Our soul whispers to us through the corridors of time, revealing the hidden patterns that shape our lives. By listening intently to these whispers, we can break free from self-limiting beliefs and embark on a path of self-discovery and empowerment.

FOUR

UNCOVER THE ROOT CAUSES OF YOUR FEARS AND ANXIETIES.

In the quiet corners of our minds, fears and anxieties often lurk, casting shadows over our present lives. These unwelcome companions can manifest in a multitude of ways, from irrational phobias and social anxieties to crippling panic attacks and persistent worries. While modern therapies offer various tools to manage these challenges, past life regression provides a unique perspective, delving into the depths of our subconscious to uncover the root causes of our fears and anxieties.

At its core, past life regression operates on the premise that our current experiences are not isolated incidents but rather echoes of previous lifetimes. The unresolved traumas, emotional wounds, and negative experiences we carry from past lives can significantly impact our present well-being, manifesting as fears and anxieties that seem irrational or inexplicable. By exploring these past experiences, we can gain profound insights into the origins of our fears, allowing us to address and heal the root causes.

One of the most common ways in which past life regression helps to uncover the root causes of fears is by identifying and releasing trapped emotions. When we experience traumatic events, the associated emotions can become trapped in our energy field, creating blockages that manifest as physical or emotional ailments. By revisiting these past experiences, we can allow these emotions to surface and be processed, releasing the energetic hold they have on us. This can lead to a significant reduction in anxiety and fear, as we no longer carry the weight of these unresolved emotions.

Past life regression can also help us to identify and heal phobias. Phobias are often irrational and intense fears of specific objects or situations, such as spiders, heights, or enclosed spaces. In many cases, these phobias can be traced back to traumatic experiences in past lives. For example, a fear of water may stem from a past life experience of drowning, or a fear of heights may be linked to a past life experience of falling from a great height. By revisiting these experiences and understanding the context in which they occurred, we can reframe our relationship with the object or situation, reducing or eliminating the fear associated with it.

Past life regression can also shed light on generalized anxiety disorder (GAD), a condition characterized by persistent and excessive worry about various aspects of life. GAD can be debilitating, affecting our ability to function in daily life. Through past life regression, we may discover that our anxieties are rooted in unresolved traumas or negative experiences from past lives. By addressing these underlying causes, we can reduce the intensity and frequency of our worries, allowing us to live a more peaceful and fulfilling life.

Another way in which past life regression can help to uncover the root causes of fears and anxieties is by identifying and releasing negative beliefs and thought patterns. Often, our fears and anxieties are fueled by deeply ingrained beliefs about ourselves and the world around us. These beliefs may have been formed in past lives based on traumatic experiences or negative self-perceptions. By exploring these beliefs and their origins, we can challenge their validity and replace them with more positive and empowering thoughts.

Past life regression can also help us to understand the role of karma in our lives. Karma, the law of cause and effect, suggests that our actions in past lives can create energetic debts or imbalances that carry over into our present incarnation. These karmic patterns can manifest as fears and anxieties, as we unconsciously carry the burden of past mistakes or unresolved conflicts. By recognizing these patterns, we can consciously choose to break free from them, making amends for past wrongs and creating a more positive trajectory for our lives.

It is important to note that past life regression is not a magic bullet for overcoming fears and anxieties. It is a tool that can be used in conjunction with other therapies and approaches, such as cognitive-behavioral therapy (CBT) and mindfulness practices. The process of healing is often gradual and requires patience, self-compassion, and a willingness to face our fears head-on.

ppp

The past is not a burden to carry, but a treasure trove of wisdom to embrace. Each life we have lived holds valuable lessons that can guide us towards a more purposeful and authentic existence.

FIVE

FIND PEACE AND RESOLUTION IN PAST LIFE CONNECTIONS.

Life's tapestry is interwoven with intricate threads of relationships, each one carrying a unique significance in our journey. Some connections feel familiar, as if we have known each other before, while others are fraught with tension and conflict. Past life regression offers a unique perspective on these relationships, unveiling the hidden connections that span across lifetimes and providing an opportunity to find peace and resolution in past life connections.

The concept of soul connections posits that we encounter certain individuals repeatedly across different lifetimes, each encounter serving a specific purpose in our soul's evolution. These connections can be romantic, familial, platonic, or even adversarial, each playing a role in our growth and learning. Past life regression allows us to explore these connections, understanding the karmic debts, soul contracts, and unresolved emotions that may be influencing our present relationships.

One of the most profound ways in which past life regression can bring peace and resolution is by understanding the karmic origins of our connections. Karma, the law of cause and effect, suggests that our actions in past lives create energetic debts or imbalances that carry over into our present incarnation. By revisiting past lives, we can gain insight into the karmic patterns that are playing out in our current relationships, recognizing the debts we owe to others and the lessons we need to learn. This understanding can lead to forgiveness, compassion, and ultimately, resolution.

Past life regression can also help us to heal past life traumas that may be impacting our current relationships. For example, if we experienced betrayal or abandonment in a past life, we may carry those wounds into our present relationships, leading to trust issues or fear of intimacy. By revisiting those past life experiences and processing the emotions associated with them, we can release the pain and create space for healing and forgiveness.

Another way in which past life regression can bring resolution is by understanding the purpose of our soul contracts. Soul contracts are agreements that we make with other souls before incarnating, outlining the lessons we wish to learn, the experiences we wish to have, and the relationships we wish to form. By recognizing these soul contracts, we can gain a deeper understanding of the purpose and meaning behind our current relationships, recognizing the challenges and opportunities they present for our soul's growth.

Past life regression can also facilitate communication and understanding between souls. By revisiting past life experiences together, we can gain insight into the dynamics of our relationship, understanding each other's motivations, fears, and desires. This can lead to greater empathy, compassion, and ultimately, a deeper connection.

In some cases, past life regression can reveal past life vows or commitments that may be influencing our current relationships. For example, if we made a vow of eternal love in a past life, we may unconsciously be seeking to fulfill that vow in our present relationship. By recognizing these past life vows and understanding their impact on our current lives, we can make conscious choices about whether to uphold or release them.

While past life regression can be a powerful tool for finding peace and resolution in past life connections, it is important to approach this practice with an open mind and a healthy dose of skepticism. Not all experiences may be accurate or meaningful, and it is important to trust your intuition and discernment when interpreting the information that emerges. It is also crucial to work with a qualified and experienced practitioner who can guide you through the process safely and effectively.

In conclusion, finding peace and resolution in past life connections is a journey of self-discovery, healing, and forgiveness. By exploring the hidden connections that span across lifetimes, we can gain profound insights into the dynamics of our relationships, heal past wounds, and create a more harmonious and fulfilling present. This journey is not always easy, but it is undoubtedly worth it. For in the process of understanding and resolving our past life connections, we open ourselves up to a deeper connection with our own soul and with the souls of those around us.

ÞÞÞ

Our soul's journey is a tapestry woven with threads of love, loss, and transformation. By exploring the depths of our past lives, we can reconnect with lost loved ones, heal old wounds, and find peace and resolution in the present.

SIX

REFRAME CHALLENGING EXPERIENCES WITH NEW UNDERSTANDING.

Life is a tapestry woven with threads of joy, sorrow, triumph, and adversity. Challenging experiences are an inevitable part of our human journey, often leaving us with scars, both physical and emotional. Yet, these experiences can also serve as catalysts for growth, offering profound lessons and opportunities for transformation. Past life regression provides a unique lens through which we can reframe these challenging experiences, gaining new understanding and ultimately finding healing and empowerment.

At its core, past life regression operates on the premise that our current experiences are not isolated incidents but rather echoes of previous lifetimes. The unresolved traumas, emotional wounds, and negative experiences we carry from past lives can significantly impact our present well-being, shaping our perceptions, beliefs, and behaviors. By delving into these past experiences, we can gain a deeper understanding of the root causes of our current challenges, allowing us to reframe them with a new perspective.

One of the most powerful ways in which past life regression helps us to reframe challenging experiences is by providing context and understanding. Often, we view our current struggles through a limited lens, focusing on the immediate circumstances and failing to see the bigger picture. By revisiting past lives, we can gain a broader perspective, recognizing that our current challenges are not random events but rather part of a larger karmic pattern or soul contract, This understanding can help us to make sense of our experiences, finding meaning and purpose in even the most difficult situations.

Past life regression can also help us to identify and release negative beliefs and thought patterns that may be contributing to our current challenges. Often, we hold onto limiting beliefs about ourselves and the world around us, based on past experiences or societal conditioning. These beliefs can create self-fulfilling prophecies, attracting experiences that reinforce our negative self-perceptions. By exploring the origins of these beliefs in past lives, we can challenge their validity and replace them with more positive and empowering thoughts.

Another way in which past life regression can reframe challenging experiences is by allowing us to see the bigger picture of our soul's journey. By understanding that our current life is just one chapter in a much larger story, we can gain a sense of perspective and resilience. We may realize that our current challenges are simply stepping stones on our path to growth and evolution, and that even the most difficult experiences can serve a higher purpose.

Past life regression can also help us to develop compassion and empathy for ourselves and others. By understanding the karmic origins of our challenges, we can recognize that we are not victims of circumstance but rather co-creators of our own reality. We can forgive ourselves for past mistakes and choose to move forward with a renewed sense of purpose and direction. This newfound compassion can also extend to others, as we recognize that everyone is on their own unique journey, facing their own challenges and learning their own lessons.

Through past life regression, we can also access the wisdom and guidance of our higher selves. By connecting with our soul's essence, we can gain valuable insights into the meaning and purpose of our experiences. This connection can provide us with a sense of peace, acceptance, and understanding, even in the face of adversity.

The process of reframing challenging experiences through past life regression is not always easy. It requires courage, vulnerability, and a willingness to face the depths of our being. However, the rewards are immeasurable. By gaining a new understanding of our past, we can heal old wounds, release limiting beliefs, and create a more fulfilling and joyful present.

As we reframe our challenging experiences, we begin to see them not as obstacles but as opportunities for growth and transformation. We learn to embrace the lessons they offer, recognizing that even the most difficult experiences can serve a higher purpose. We develop resilience, compassion, and a deeper understanding of ourselves and the world around us.

In conclusion, past life regression offers a powerful tool for reframing challenging experiences with new understanding. By exploring our past lives, we can gain profound insights into the root causes of our current challenges, allowing us to heal old wounds, release limiting beliefs, and create a more positive and empowering narrative for our lives. This journey is not always easy, but it is undoubtedly worth it. For in the process of reframing our past, we open ourselves up to a future of infinite possibilities.

ϷϷϷ

The echoes of our past lives are not mere whispers, but powerful vibrations that can reshape our present reality. By harnessing the transformative power of past life regression, we can create lasting change and step into our full potential.

SEVEN

TRANSFORM YOUR RELATIONSHIPS THROUGH FORGIVENESS AND COMPASSION.

Relationships are the cornerstone of human existence, shaping our experiences, influencing our growth, and providing a canvas for both joy and sorrow. Yet, often these connections are fraught with misunderstandings, conflicts, and unresolved emotions that can hinder our ability to form deep and meaningful bonds. Past life regression offers a unique lens through which we can transform our relationships, fostering forgiveness, compassion, and understanding.

At its core, past life regression operates on the premise that our current relationships are not isolated incidents but rather a continuation of connections that have spanned across multiple lifetimes. The unresolved conflicts, emotional wounds, and karmic debts from past lives can significantly impact our present relationships, creating patterns of dysfunction and disharmony. By exploring these past life connections, we can gain a deeper understanding of the root causes of our current relationship challenges, allowing us to heal old wounds and create a more harmonious and fulfilling present.

One of the most powerful ways in which past life regression can transform our relationships is by fostering forgiveness. Often, we carry grudges, resentments, and anger towards others, stemming from past hurts or perceived injustices. These negative emotions can poison our relationships, creating a cycle of conflict and pain. By revisiting past lives, we can gain a new perspective on these events, understanding the motivations and circumstances that led to the hurtful actions. This understanding can open the door to forgiveness, allowing us to release the negative emotions that have been holding us back and move forward with compassion and understanding.

Past life regression can also help us to cultivate compassion for ourselves and others. By recognizing that we are all on a journey of growth and evolution, making mistakes and learning from them along the way, we can develop a more forgiving and accepting attitude towards ourselves and others. This shift in perspective can profoundly impact our relationships, allowing us to see beyond the surface-level conflicts and connect with the deeper essence of each other's souls.

Another way in which past life regression can transform our relationships is by identifying and releasing karmic patterns. Karma, the law of cause and effect, suggests that our actions in past lives can create energetic debts or imbalances that carry over into our present incarnation. These karmic patterns can manifest in various ways in our relationships, such as repeating the same dysfunctional dynamics or attracting partners who trigger our unresolved emotional wounds. By recognizing these patterns, we can consciously choose to break free from them, making amends for past mistakes and creating a more positive and harmonious future for ourselves and our loved ones.

Past life regression can also facilitate communication and understanding between souls. By revisiting past life experiences together, we can gain insight into the dynamics of our relationship, understanding each other's motivations, fears, and desires. This can lead to deeper empathy, compassion, and ultimately, a stronger bond.

In some cases, past life regression can reveal past life vows or commitments that may be influencing our current relationships. For example, if we made a vow of eternal love in a past life, we may unconsciously be seeking to fulfill that vow in our present relationship. By recognizing these past life vows and understanding their impact on our current lives, we can make conscious choices about whether to uphold or release them, creating a more authentic and fulfilling connection.

The process of transforming our relationships through forgiveness and compassion is not always easy. It requires a willingness to confront our own shadows, to acknowledge our own role in creating conflict, and to let go of the need to be right. However, the rewards are immeasurable. By releasing the burdens of the past and embracing forgiveness and compassion, we can create deeper, more meaningful connections with others, fostering a sense of love, trust, and understanding that can enrich our lives in countless ways.

In conclusion, past life regression offers a powerful tool for transforming our relationships through forgiveness and compassion. By exploring our past life connections, we can heal old wounds, release karmic patterns, and cultivate a deeper understanding of ourselves and others. This journey is not always easy, but it is undoubtedly worth it. For in the process of transforming our relationships, we open ourselves up to a more loving, compassionate, and interconnected world.

ϷϷϷ

Our soul's journey is a sacred dance, a rhythmic flow of experiences that shape our understanding of ourselves and the world around us. Through past life regression, we can learn the steps to this dance, allowing us to move through life with grace, purpose, and joy.

EIGHT

AWAKEN TO YOUR SOUL'S PURPOSE AND POTENTIAL.

In the depths of our being lies a profound yearning for purpose, a desire to understand our unique place in the grand tapestry of existence. We long to know why we are here, what we are meant to contribute, and how we can fulfill our highest potential. Past life regression offers a powerful tool for awakening to our soul's purpose and potential, unveiling the hidden truths that lie dormant within us.

At its core, past life regression operates on the premise that our current life is not an isolated incident but rather a continuation of a larger narrative that spans across multiple lifetimes. The experiences, lessons, and talents we have accumulated over countless lifetimes are imprinted on our soul, shaping our desires, motivations, and potential in the present. By delving into these past lives, we can gain valuable insights into our soul's journey, recognizing the recurring themes, patterns, and gifts that have been woven into the fabric of our being.

One of the most profound ways in which past life regression can awaken us to our soul's purpose is by revealing our past life passions and talents. We may discover that we were artists, healers, teachers, or warriors in previous incarnations, carrying those skills and inclinations into our present lives. By recognizing and embracing these innate gifts, we can unlock our full potential and find fulfillment in activities that resonate with our soul's deepest desires.

Past life regression can also help us to understand the karmic lessons we are here to learn. Karma, the law of cause and effect, suggests that our actions in past lives create energetic debts or imbalances that carry over into our present incarnation. By revisiting past lives, we can gain insight into these karmic patterns, recognizing the challenges we have chosen to overcome and the lessons we need to learn in this lifetime. This understanding can empower us to embrace our challenges with greater purpose and clarity, recognizing them as opportunities for growth and transformation.

Another way in which past life regression can awaken us to our soul's purpose is by revealing our soul contracts or agreements. These are agreements that we make with other souls before incarnating, outlining the lessons we wish to learn, the experiences we wish to have, and the relationships we wish to form. By recognizing these soul contracts, we can gain a deeper understanding of our life's purpose and the unique role we are meant to play in the world.

Past life regression can also help us to connect with our spirit guides and higher selves. These wise and benevolent beings are always available to offer guidance and support, but we may not always be aware of their presence. By delving into our past lives, we can open ourselves up to their guidance, receiving messages and insights that can help us to navigate our current challenges and fulfill our soul's mission.

Through past life regression, we can also develop a deeper understanding of our own soul's essence. By revisiting past lives, we can witness the evolution of our soul across time, recognizing the recurring themes, patterns, and lessons that have shaped our journey. This understanding can help us to connect with our deepest values, beliefs, and aspirations, aligning our lives with our soul's true purpose.

The process of awakening to our soul's purpose and potential through past life regression is not always easy. It requires a willingness to confront our shadows, to let go of limiting beliefs, and to embrace the unknown. However, the rewards are immeasurable. By discovering our true purpose and potential, we can live a more authentic, fulfilling, and joyful life, aligned with our soul's deepest desires.

As we awaken to our soul's purpose, we begin to see the world through a new lens. We recognize the interconnectedness of all things, the beauty and complexity of life's tapestry, and our own unique role in the grand scheme of things. We become more compassionate, more loving, and more connected to our true selves and to the world around us.

In conclusion, past life regression offers a powerful tool for awakening to our soul's purpose and potential. By delving into our past lives, we can gain valuable insights into our soul's journey, recognizing the recurring themes, patterns, and gifts that have shaped our being. We can uncover our hidden talents, understand our karmic lessons, and connect with our spirit guides and higher selves. This journey of self-discovery and empowerment can lead us to a more authentic, fulfilling, and joyful life, aligned with our soul's deepest desires.

ᐧᐧᐧ

The past is not a prison, but a portal to deeper understanding. By venturing through this portal, we can uncover the root causes of our fears and anxieties, freeing ourselves from the shackles of the past and embracing a life of greater peace and fulfillment.

NINE

RECONNECT WITH LOST LOVED ONES AND SPIRIT GUIDES.

Life's journey is often marked by both joyful reunions and painful separations. The loss of loved ones can leave a void in our hearts, a longing for connection that transcends the physical realm. Similarly, we may yearn for guidance and support from spiritual mentors or guides who can illuminate our path. Past life regression offers a unique pathway to reconnect with lost loved ones and spirit guides, bridging the gap between the physical and spiritual dimensions and fostering healing, closure, and renewed connection.

The concept of reincarnation, central to past life regression, posits that our souls embark on multiple lifetimes, each one offering opportunities for growth, learning, and connection. The relationships we form in these lifetimes are not limited to a single incarnation but can extend across multiple lifetimes. Through past life regression, we can tap into these soul connections, revisiting past lives where we shared deep bonds with loved ones who have since passed on.

By revisiting these past life experiences, we can gain a deeper understanding of the nature of our relationships with loved ones. We may discover shared experiences, unresolved conflicts, or karmic patterns that have carried over into our present lives. This understanding can provide closure, allowing us to heal old wounds, forgive past transgressions, and move forward with a renewed sense of peace and acceptance.

Past life regression can also facilitate communication with loved ones who have passed on. While the experience may not be the same as a physical conversation, it can provide a sense of comfort and reassurance, knowing that our loved ones are still with us in spirit. We may receive messages of love, guidance, or support, helping us to navigate our current challenges and find peace in our grief.

In addition to reconnecting with lost loved ones, past life regression can also help us to connect with our spirit guides. Spirit guides are non-physical beings who offer guidance, support, and protection throughout our soul's journey. They may be ascended masters, angels, ancestors, or other benevolent beings who have chosen to assist us in our spiritual growth.

By accessing past life experiences, we can often identify the spirit guides who have been with us throughout our many lifetimes. We may recognize familiar faces, hear comforting voices, or feel a sense of warmth and love surrounding us. This connection can provide us with a sense of comfort and reassurance, knowing that we are not alone on our journey.

Through past life regression, we can also deepen our connection with our spirit guides, learning to trust their guidance and wisdom. We may receive messages, insights, or intuitive nudges that can help us to navigate our current challenges and make choices that are aligned with our highest good. This connection can be incredibly empowering, providing us with the support and guidance we need to overcome obstacles and fulfill our soul's purpose.

It is important to note that reconnecting with lost loved ones and spirit guides through past life regression is a deeply personal and subjective experience. Not everyone may have the same experience, and it is important to trust your own intuition and discernment when interpreting the information that emerges. It is also crucial to work with a qualified and experienced practitioner who can guide you through the process safely and effectively.

In conclusion, past life regression offers a unique and powerful way to reconnect with lost loved ones and spirit guides. By exploring our past lives, we can tap into the deep soul connections that transcend the boundaries of time and space. We can gain closure, healing, and renewed connection with loved ones who have passed on, and we can deepen our relationship with our spirit guides, receiving their guidance and support on our life's journey. This journey of reconnection can be incredibly transformative, offering comfort, healing, and a renewed sense of purpose and direction.

ɔɔɔ

Our soul's journey is a symphony of interconnected lives, each one contributing to the grand melody of our existence. Through past life regression, we can hear the harmonies of our past, present, and future, creating a life that resonates with our true essence.

TEN

GAIN CLARITY ON YOUR LIFE'S PATH AND DIRECTION.

Life's journey can often feel like navigating a winding road with unclear directions and unexpected turns. The path ahead may seem obscured, leaving us unsure of which direction to take. In these moments of uncertainty, we yearn for clarity and guidance, seeking a deeper understanding of our purpose and the path we are meant to follow. Past life regression offers a unique tool for gaining this clarity, illuminating our life's path and direction through the exploration of past lives.

The premise of past life regression is that our current life is not an isolated incident but rather a continuation of a larger narrative that spans across multiple lifetimes. The choices we made, the experiences we had, and the lessons we learned in previous incarnations have left indelible imprints on our soul, shaping our desires, motivations, and potential in the present. By delving into these past lives, we can gain valuable insights into the recurring themes, patterns, and unresolved issues that may be influencing our current life path.

One of the most powerful ways in which past life regression can bring clarity is by revealing our soul's purpose and mission. Through exploring past lives, we may discover a recurring theme or passion that has carried over from lifetime to lifetime. This could be a deep-seated desire to heal others, a talent for creativity, or a calling to leadership. By recognizing these patterns, we can gain a deeper understanding of our soul's purpose and the unique gifts we have to offer the world. This clarity can guide us in making decisions about our career, relationships, and personal pursuits, aligning our actions with our true calling.

Past life regression can also help us to identify and overcome obstacles and challenges that are hindering our progress. By revisiting past lives, we may discover unresolved conflicts, traumas, or negative patterns that are still influencing our present lives. For example, a fear of public speaking may stem from a past life experience of being ridiculed or shamed. By understanding the root cause of this fear, we can take steps to heal the underlying trauma and move forward with confidence.

Another way in which past life regression can provide clarity is by revealing our soul contracts or agreements. These are agreements that we make with other souls before incarnating, outlining the lessons we wish to learn, the experiences we wish to have, and the relationships we wish to form. By recognizing these soul contracts, we can gain a deeper understanding of the purpose and meaning behind our current life circumstances. We may realize that certain challenges or relationships are part of our soul's pre-determined plan, offering us valuable opportunities for growth and learning.

Past life regression can also help us to connect with our spirit guides and higher selves. These wise and benevolent beings offer guidance and support throughout our soul's journey. By accessing past life experiences, we can often identify the spirit guides who have been with us throughout our many lifetimes. We may recognize familiar faces, hear comforting voices, or feel a sense of warmth and love surrounding us. This connection can provide us with a sense of comfort and reassurance, knowing that we are not alone on our journey.

Through past life regression, we can also develop a deeper understanding of our own intuition and inner guidance. By revisiting past lives where we made choices that led to positive outcomes, we can strengthen our trust in our own inner wisdom. This can empower us to make decisions that are aligned with our true desires and values, even when faced with uncertainty or external pressures.

It is important to note that gaining clarity on our life's path and direction through past life regression is not a quick fix or a magic bullet. It is a process of self-discovery and exploration that requires patience, openness, and a willingness to confront our shadows. It is also important to work with a qualified and experienced practitioner who can guide you through the process safely and effectively.

In conclusion, past life regression offers a unique and powerful tool for gaining clarity on our life's path and direction. By exploring our past lives, we can uncover our soul's purpose, identify and overcome obstacles, understand our soul contracts, and connect with our spirit guides and higher selves. This journey of self-discovery can empower us to make choices that are aligned with our true desires and values, leading us to a more fulfilling, purposeful, and joyful life.

ββ β

The past is not a burden, but a bridge to our future. By crossing this bridge, we can gain clarity on our life's path and direction, making choices that align with our soul's purpose and leading to a more fulfilling and joyful present.

ELEVEN

BREAK FREE FROM LIMITING BELIEFS AND SELF-SABOTAGE.

Life is a symphony of choices, actions, and consequences, yet often we find ourselves trapped in repetitive cycles of self-defeating behavior and limiting beliefs. We may sabotage our relationships, careers, or personal goals, seemingly unable to break free from the invisible chains that bind us. Past life regression offers a profound opportunity to delve into the roots of these self-destructive patterns, uncovering their origins in past lives and empowering us to create lasting change.

The concept of past life regression is grounded in the understanding that our present lives are not isolated incidents but rather continuations of a larger narrative that spans across multiple lifetimes. The unresolved traumas, emotional wounds, and negative experiences we carry from past lives can significantly impact our present well-being, manifesting as limiting beliefs and self-sabotaging behaviors. By exploring these past experiences, we can gain valuable insights into the root causes of our self-defeating patterns, allowing us to break free from their grip and embrace a more empowered and fulfilling life.

One of the most common ways in which past life regression helps us to break free from limiting beliefs is by identifying and challenging their origins. Often, our limiting beliefs are formed in childhood or through negative experiences in our current life. However, past life regression can reveal that these beliefs may have deeper roots, originating in traumatic events or negative self-perceptions from previous incarnations. By revisiting these past experiences, we can understand the context in which these beliefs were formed and recognize that they are not absolute truths but rather subjective interpretations of events. This realization can empower us to challenge these beliefs and replace them with more positive and empowering thoughts.

Past life regression can also help us to identify and release karmic patterns that contribute to self-sabotage. Karma, the law of cause and effect, suggests that our actions in past lives can create energetic debts or imbalances that carry over into our present incarnation. These karmic patterns can manifest as self-destructive behaviors, such as addiction, procrastination, or fear of success. By recognizing these patterns, we can consciously choose to break free from them, making amends for past mistakes and creating a more positive trajectory for our lives.

Another way in which past life regression can empower us to break free from self-sabotage is by revealing our soul contracts or agreements. These are agreements that we make with other souls before incarnating, outlining the lessons we wish to learn, the experiences we wish to have, and the relationships we wish to form. Sometimes, these soul contracts can involve challenging experiences or obstacles that are designed to help us grow and evolve. By understanding the purpose of these challenges, we can approach them with greater courage and determination, recognizing them as opportunities for growth rather than setbacks.

Past life regression can also help us to connect with our inner wisdom and intuition. By accessing the vast knowledge and experience we have accumulated over countless lifetimes, we can gain valuable insights into our own strengths, weaknesses, and potential. This connection to our inner wisdom can empower us to make choices that are aligned with our true desires and values, rather than being driven by fear or self-doubt.

The process of breaking free from limiting beliefs and self-sabotage through past life regression is not always easy. It requires a willingness to confront our shadows, to acknowledge our own responsibility for our choices and actions, and to embrace the unknown. However, the rewards are immeasurable. By releasing the shackles of self-limiting beliefs and behaviors, we can create a life of greater freedom, joy, and fulfillment.

As we break free from self-sabotage, we begin to see ourselves and the world around us with new eyes. We recognize our own worthiness, our own potential, and our own power to create the life we desire. We embrace our challenges as opportunities for growth, and we trust in our own inner guidance to lead us towards our highest good.

In conclusion, past life regression offers a profound opportunity to break free from limiting beliefs and self-sabotage. By exploring our past lives, we can gain valuable insights into the root causes of our self-defeating patterns, allowing us to heal old wounds, release karmic patterns, and connect with our inner wisdom. This journey of self-discovery and empowerment can lead us to a life of greater freedom, joy, and fulfillment.

ᎮᎮᎮ

Our soul's journey is a treasure map, guiding us towards the hidden treasures within ourselves. Through past life regression, we can decipher the clues of our past, unlocking the door to our full potential and embracing a life of purpose.

TWELVE

RELEASE EMOTIONAL BAGGAGE AND RECLAIM YOUR POWER.

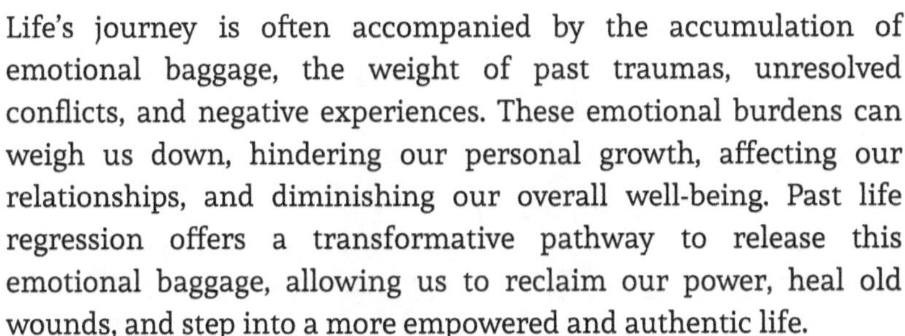

Life's journey is often accompanied by the accumulation of emotional baggage, the weight of past traumas, unresolved conflicts, and negative experiences. These emotional burdens can weigh us down, hindering our personal growth, affecting our relationships, and diminishing our overall well-being. Past life regression offers a transformative pathway to release this emotional baggage, allowing us to reclaim our power, heal old wounds, and step into a more empowered and authentic life.

The concept of past life regression is rooted in the understanding that our current lives are not isolated incidents but rather continuations of a larger narrative that spans across multiple lifetimes. The unresolved emotions and traumas we carry from past lives can significantly impact our present well-being, manifesting as anxiety, depression, anger, or other emotional challenges. By delving into these past experiences, we can gain valuable insights into the root causes of our emotional baggage, allowing us to address and heal the underlying wounds.

One of the most powerful ways in which past life regression helps us to release emotional baggage is by providing a safe and supportive space to process and release trapped emotions. Often, we suppress or bury our emotions, fearing the pain or vulnerability that comes with facing them. However, these unprocessed emotions can fester and manifest in unhealthy ways, such as physical ailments or self-destructive behaviors. Through past life regression, we can revisit the past experiences that triggered these emotions, allowing ourselves to feel them fully and release them in a safe and controlled environment. This process of emotional release can be incredibly cathartic, freeing us from the weight of past traumas and allowing us to move forward with a renewed sense of lightness and freedom.

Past life regression can also help us to identify and reframe negative beliefs and thought patterns that contribute to our emotional baggage. Often, we hold onto limiting beliefs about ourselves, others, or the world around us, based on past experiences or societal conditioning. These beliefs can create self-fulfilling prophecies, attracting experiences that reinforce our negative self-perceptions. By exploring the origins of these beliefs in past lives, we can challenge their validity and replace them with more positive and empowering thoughts. This shift in perspective can profoundly impact our emotional well-being, allowing us to break free from the cycle of negativity and embrace a more optimistic and hopeful outlook.

Another way in which past life regression can help us to release emotional baggage is by identifying and resolving karmic patterns.

Karma, the law of cause and effect, suggests that our actions in past lives can create energetic debts or imbalances that carry over into our present incarnation. These karmic patterns can manifest as recurring challenges, conflicts, or negative emotions in our lives. By recognizing these patterns, we can consciously choose to break free from them, making amends for past mistakes and creating a more positive trajectory for our lives. This can lead to a profound sense of liberation and empowerment, as we release the burdens of the past and embrace the freedom to create a new future.

Through past life regression, we can also reconnect with our inner strength and resilience. By revisiting past lives where we overcame challenges, adversity, or trauma, we can tap into the inherent strength and wisdom that lies within us. This can empower us to face our current challenges with greater courage and determination, recognizing that we have the inner resources to overcome any obstacle.

The process of releasing emotional baggage and reclaiming our power through past life regression is not always easy. It requires a willingness to confront our shadows, to acknowledge our own vulnerabilities, and to embrace the unknown. However, the rewards are immeasurable. By releasing the burdens of the past, we can create space for joy, love, and authentic expression.

As we reclaim our power, we begin to see ourselves and the world around us with new eyes. We recognize our own worthiness, our own potential, and our own capacity for love and happiness. We embrace our challenges as opportunities for growth, and we trust in our own inner guidance to lead us towards our highest good.

In conclusion, past life regression offers a transformative pathway to release emotional baggage and reclaim our power. By exploring our past lives, we can gain valuable insights into the root causes of our emotional burdens, allowing us to heal old wounds, reframe negative beliefs, and break free from karmic patterns. This journey of self-discovery and empowerment can lead us to a more authentic, joyful, and fulfilling life, where we are free to express our true selves and create the reality we desire.

ϷϷϷ

*The past is not a closed book, but an open invitation
to explore the mysteries of our soul. By turning the
pages of our past lives, we can discover the wisdom
and lessons that will empower us to create a more
fulfilling and joyful present.*

THIRTEEN

CULTIVATE INNER PEACE AND SELF-LOVE THROUGH PAST LIFE HEALING.

In our modern world, the pursuit of inner peace and self-love often feels like an elusive quest. We are bombarded with external pressures, expectations, and distractions that can lead us astray from our true selves. Past life healing offers a unique pathway to cultivate inner peace and self-love, allowing us to connect with our soul's essence, heal old wounds, and embrace our inherent worthiness.

At its core, past life healing operates on the premise that our current experiences are not isolated incidents but rather continuations of a larger narrative that spans across multiple lifetimes. The unresolved traumas, emotional wounds, and negative experiences we carry from past lives can significantly impact our present well-being, hindering our ability to cultivate inner peace and self-love. By delving into these past experiences, we can gain valuable insights into the root causes of our self-doubt, insecurity, and negative self-talk, allowing us to address and heal the underlying wounds.

One of the most powerful ways in which past life healing fosters inner peace is by resolving past life traumas. Traumatic experiences can leave deep emotional scars that continue to affect us in the present, even if we are not consciously aware of them. These traumas can manifest as anxiety, depression, phobias, or other emotional challenges. By revisiting these past life experiences in a safe and supportive environment, we can process the emotions associated with them, release the trauma from our energy field, and create space for healing and peace.

Past life healing can also help us to cultivate self-love by identifying and releasing negative beliefs and thought patterns that have been ingrained in us from past lives. Often, we carry limiting beliefs about ourselves, based on past experiences or societal conditioning. These beliefs can lead to self-doubt, insecurity, and a lack of self-worth. By exploring the origins of these beliefs in past lives, we can challenge their validity and replace them with more positive and empowering thoughts. This shift in perspective can profoundly impact our relationship with ourselves, allowing us to embrace our true worth and cultivate a deeper sense of self-love.

Another way in which past life healing fosters inner peace is by releasing karmic burdens. Karma, the law of cause and effect, suggests that our actions in past lives can create energetic debts or imbalances that carry over into our present incarnation. These karmic burdens can manifest as guilt, shame, or a sense of unworthiness. By revisiting past lives and understanding the karmic patterns that have been playing out in our lives, we can consciously choose to break free from them, making amends for past mistakes and creating a more positive trajectory for our lives.

This can lead to a profound sense of liberation and inner peace, as we release the burdens of the past and embrace the freedom to create a new future.

Past life healing can also help us to connect with our higher selves and inner wisdom. By accessing the vast knowledge and experience we have accumulated over countless lifetimes, we can gain valuable insights into our own strengths, weaknesses, and potential. This connection to our higher self can provide us with a sense of peace, clarity, and direction, allowing us to make choices that are aligned with our true values and aspirations.

The process of cultivating inner peace and self-love through past life healing is not always easy. It requires a willingness to confront our shadows, to acknowledge our own vulnerabilities, and to embrace the unknown. However, the rewards are immeasurable. By healing old wounds, releasing negative beliefs, and reconnecting with our inner wisdom, we can create a life of greater peace, joy, and fulfillment.

As we cultivate inner peace and self-love, we begin to see ourselves and the world around us with new eyes. We recognize the inherent beauty and goodness in all things, including ourselves. We develop a deeper sense of compassion for ourselves and others, and we learn to embrace our imperfections as part of our human experience.

ᕹᕹᕹ

Our soul's journey is a pilgrimage, a sacred quest for self-discovery and healing. Through past life regression, we can walk this path with greater awareness and understanding, allowing us to transform our lives and step into our full potential.

FOURTEEN

EMBRACE THE WISDOM AND LESSONS OF YOUR PAST LIVES.

Life is a tapestry woven with countless threads, each representing a unique experience, lesson, or encounter. While we often focus on the present moment, the echoes of our past lives resonate within us, carrying wisdom and insights that can profoundly shape our understanding of ourselves and the world around us. Past life regression offers a unique opportunity to tap into this vast reservoir of knowledge, allowing us to embrace the wisdom and lessons of our past lives and integrate them into our present existence.

The concept of reincarnation, central to past life regression, suggests that our souls embark on multiple lifetimes, each one offering a unique set of experiences and challenges. Through the process of reincarnation, we accumulate a wealth of knowledge and wisdom that transcends the boundaries of a single lifetime. By accessing these past lives, we can tap into this vast reservoir of wisdom, gaining valuable insights into our own patterns, behaviors, and tendencies.

One of the most profound ways in which past life regression allows us to embrace the wisdom of our past lives is by revealing the recurring themes and patterns that have shaped our soul's journey. We may discover that we have repeatedly faced similar challenges, made similar mistakes, or attracted similar types of relationships across multiple lifetimes. By recognizing these patterns, we can gain a deeper understanding of our own tendencies and motivations, allowing us to make more conscious choices in the present.

Past life regression can also help us to understand the karmic lessons we are here to learn. Karma, the law of cause and effect, suggests that our actions in past lives create energetic debts or imbalances that carry over into our present incarnation. By revisiting past lives, we can gain insight into these karmic patterns, recognizing the challenges we have chosen to overcome and the lessons we need to learn in this lifetime. This understanding can empower us to embrace our challenges with greater purpose and clarity, recognizing them as opportunities for growth and transformation.

Another way in which past life regression can help us to embrace the wisdom of our past lives is by revealing our soul's purpose and mission. Through exploring past lives, we may discover a recurring theme or passion that has carried over from lifetime to lifetime. This could be a deep-seated desire to heal others, a talent for creativity, or a calling to leadership. By recognizing these patterns, we can gain a deeper understanding of our soul's purpose and the unique gifts we have to offer the world. This clarity can guide us in making decisions about our career, relationships, and personal pursuits, aligning our actions with our true calling.

Past life regression can also help us to connect with our spirit guides and higher selves. These wise and benevolent beings offer guidance and support throughout our soul's journey. By accessing past life experiences, we can often identify the spirit guides who have been with us throughout our many lifetimes. We may recognize familiar faces, hear comforting voices, or feel a sense of warmth and love surrounding us. This connection can provide us with a sense of comfort and reassurance, knowing that we are not alone on our journey.

Through past life regression, we can also develop a deeper understanding of our own intuition and inner guidance. By revisiting past lives where we made choices that led to positive outcomes, we can strengthen our trust in our own inner wisdom. This can empower us to make decisions that are aligned with our true desires and values, even when faced with uncertainty or external pressures.

The process of embracing the wisdom and lessons of our past lives through past life regression is not always easy. It requires a willingness to confront our shadows, to acknowledge our own responsibility for our choices and actions, and to embrace the unknown. However, the rewards are immeasurable. By integrating the wisdom of our past lives into our present existence, we can gain a deeper understanding of ourselves, our purpose, and our place in the world.

As we embrace the lessons of our past lives, we begin to see our current challenges and experiences in a new light. We recognize that we are not victims of circumstance but rather co-creators of our own reality. We understand that every experience, both positive and negative, serves a purpose in our soul's evolution. This understanding can empower us to live a more conscious, intentional, and fulfilling life, aligned with our highest potential.

In conclusion, past life regression offers a profound opportunity to embrace the wisdom and lessons of our past lives. By exploring our past experiences, we can gain valuable insights into our own patterns, behaviors, and tendencies. We can understand our karmic lessons, connect with our spirit guides and higher selves, and develop a deeper trust in our own intuition. This journey of self-discovery and growth can lead us to a more conscious, intentional, and fulfilling life, where we embrace our challenges as opportunities for learning and transformation.

ϼϼϼ

The past is not a ghost that haunts us, but a guiding light that illuminates our path. By embracing the wisdom of our past lives, we can break free from self-limiting beliefs and create a life of greater joy, love, and fulfillment.

FIFTEEN

CREATE A MORE FULFILLING AND JOYFUL PRESENT.

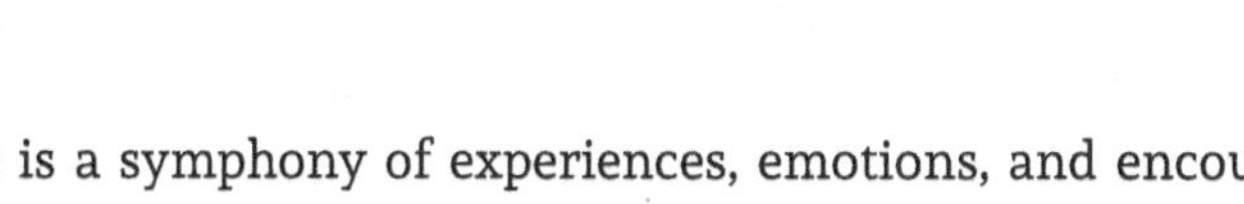

Life is a symphony of experiences, emotions, and encounters that shape our present reality. Yet, the past, with its unresolved traumas, emotional baggage, and limiting beliefs, can cast a shadow over our present, hindering our ability to fully embrace joy and fulfillment. Past life regression offers a transformative pathway to heal the wounds of the past, break free from self-limiting patterns, and create a more vibrant and joyful present.

At its core, past life regression operates on the premise that our current life is not an isolated incident but rather a continuation of a larger narrative that spans across multiple lifetimes. The unresolved emotions, traumas, and karmic patterns we carry from past lives can significantly impact our present well-being, influencing our relationships, careers, and overall happiness. By delving into these past experiences, we can gain valuable insights into the root causes of our current challenges, allowing us to heal, transform, and create a more fulfilling and joyful present.

One of the most powerful ways in which past life regression can enhance our present lives is by releasing the emotional baggage that we carry from past lives. Traumatic experiences, unresolved conflicts, and negative emotions can weigh us down, creating a sense of heaviness and stagnation. By revisiting these past experiences in a safe and supportive environment, we can process the emotions associated with them, allowing them to release their grip on us. This emotional release can lead to a profound sense of lightness and freedom, opening up space for joy, gratitude, and inner peace.

Past life regression can also help us to identify and reframe limiting beliefs that are hindering our happiness and fulfillment. Often, we carry beliefs about ourselves, others, or the world around us that are based on past experiences or societal conditioning. These beliefs can create self-fulfilling prophecies, attracting experiences that reinforce our negative self-perceptions. By exploring the origins of these beliefs in past lives, we can challenge their validity and replace them with more positive and empowering thoughts. This shift in perspective can profoundly impact our present lives, opening us up to new possibilities and opportunities.

Another way in which past life regression can enhance our present is by resolving past life conflicts and relationships. We may discover that we have unresolved conflicts or karmic debts with individuals in our current lives that stem from past life interactions. By revisiting these past life experiences, we can gain a deeper understanding of the dynamics of these relationships and find ways to heal and resolve them in the present. This can lead to deeper, more meaningful connections with others, fostering a sense of love, trust, and understanding.

Past life regression can also help us to discover our soul's purpose and passion. Often, we feel lost or unfulfilled in our lives, unsure of our direction or purpose. By exploring past lives, we may discover recurring themes, passions, or talents that have carried over from lifetime to lifetime. This can provide us with valuable clues about our true calling, inspiring us to pursue activities that align with our soul's deepest desires.

Through past life regression, we can also connect with our inner wisdom and intuition, gaining access to a wellspring of knowledge and guidance that can help us to navigate our present lives with greater clarity and purpose. By tapping into this inner wisdom, we can make choices that are aligned with our highest good, leading to a more fulfilling and joyful existence.

It is important to note that creating a more fulfilling and joyful present through past life regression is not an overnight process. It requires a willingness to confront our shadows, to explore our past with an open heart and mind, and to embrace the lessons that our experiences have to offer. However, the rewards are immeasurable. By healing the wounds of the past, we can create a more vibrant, joyful, and meaningful present, where we are free to express our true selves and live a life that is aligned with our soul's purpose.

In conclusion, past life regression offers a powerful tool for creating a more fulfilling and joyful present. By exploring our past lives, we can release emotional baggage, reframe limiting beliefs, resolve past life conflicts, discover our soul's purpose, and connect with our inner wisdom. This journey of self-discovery and healing can empower us to live a more authentic, joyful, and purposeful life, where we are free to embrace our true potential and create the reality we desire.

ᐅᐅᐅ

Our soul's journey is a kaleidoscope of experiences, each one contributing to the vibrant tapestry of our existence. Through past life regression, we can see the beauty and complexity of our soul's evolution, allowing us to embrace the fullness of who we are.

SIXTEEN

EXPERIENCE PROFOUND HEALING AND TRANSFORMATION.

Life's journey is often marked by trials, tribulations, and deep-seated wounds that can leave lasting scars on our hearts and minds. We carry the weight of past traumas, emotional baggage, and unresolved conflicts, which can hinder our ability to fully embrace joy, love, and fulfillment. Past life regression offers a transformative pathway to delve into these hidden layers of our being, facilitating profound healing and lasting transformation.

At its core, past life regression operates on the premise that our current life is not an isolated incident but rather a continuation of a larger narrative that spans across multiple lifetimes. The unresolved traumas, emotional wounds, and negative experiences we carry from past lives can significantly impact our present well-being, manifesting as physical ailments, emotional challenges, or self-limiting beliefs. By revisiting these past experiences, we can gain a deeper understanding of the root causes of our current struggles, allowing us to address and heal the underlying wounds.

One of the most profound ways in which past life regression can facilitate healing is by releasing trapped emotions. When we experience traumatic events, the associated emotions can become trapped in our energy field, creating blockages that manifest as physical or emotional ailments. By revisiting these past experiences in a safe and supportive environment, we can allow these emotions to surface and be processed, releasing the energetic hold they have on us. This emotional release can lead to a profound sense of relief and liberation, freeing us from the weight of past traumas and opening up space for healing and transformation.

Past life regression can also help us to identify and reframe negative beliefs and thought patterns that may be contributing to our current challenges. Often, we hold onto limiting beliefs about ourselves, others, or the world around us, based on past experiences or societal conditioning. These beliefs can create self-fulfilling prophecies, attracting experiences that reinforce our negative self-perceptions. By exploring the origins of these beliefs in past lives, we can challenge their validity and replace them with more positive and empowering thoughts. This shift in perspective can profoundly impact our present lives, opening us up to new possibilities and opportunities.

Another way in which past life regression can facilitate healing is by resolving past life conflicts and relationships. We may discover that we have unresolved conflicts or karmic debts with individuals in our current lives that stem from past life interactions. By revisiting these past life experiences, we can gain a deeper understanding of the dynamics of these relationships and find ways to heal and resolve them in the present. This can lead to deeper, more meaningful connections with others, fostering a sense of forgiveness, compassion, and understanding.

Past life regression can also help us to heal physical ailments that have a psychosomatic origin. Some physical ailments may be rooted in emotional traumas or unresolved conflicts from past lives. By revisiting these past experiences and processing the associated emotions, we can release the energetic blockages that are contributing to the physical ailment, allowing the body to heal itself.

The process of healing and transformation through past life regression is not always easy. It requires a willingness to confront our shadows, to acknowledge our own vulnerabilities, and to embrace the unknown. However, the rewards are immeasurable. By healing the wounds of the past, we can create a more vibrant, joyful, and meaningful present, where we are free to express our true selves and live a life that is aligned with our soul's purpose.

As we delve into the depths of our past lives, we may uncover hidden talents, passions, and gifts that we have carried with us across lifetimes. This newfound awareness can inspire us to pursue new paths, explore new possibilities, and live a more authentic and fulfilling life.

Through past life regression, we can also connect with our spirit guides and higher selves, gaining access to a wellspring of wisdom and guidance that can help us to navigate our current challenges and make choices that are aligned with our highest good. This connection can provide us with a sense of peace, acceptance, and understanding, even in the face of adversity.

In conclusion, past life regression offers a transformative pathway to experience profound healing and transformation. By exploring our past lives, we can release trapped emotions, heal old wounds, reframe negative beliefs, resolve past life conflicts, and connect with our inner wisdom. This journey of self-discovery and healing can empower us to live a more authentic, joyful, and purposeful life, where we are free to embrace our true potential and create the reality we desire.

ϷϷϷ

The past is not a prison, but a schoolhouse where we learn the lessons that will empower us to live a more fulfilling and joyful present. By revisiting these lessons, we can graduate from the school of life with greater wisdom, compassion, and understanding.

SEVENTEEN

STEP INTO YOUR FULL POTENTIAL AND LIVE A LIFE OF PURPOSE.

Life is a tapestry of experiences, woven with threads of dreams, aspirations, and untapped potential. Yet, many of us find ourselves wandering through life, feeling unfulfilled, disconnected, and uncertain about our purpose. We may yearn for a deeper meaning, a sense of direction, and a way to unleash our full potential. Past life regression offers a transformative pathway to step into our true power and live a life of purpose, revealing the hidden truths that lie dormant within us.

At its core, past life regression operates on the premise that our current life is not an isolated incident but rather a continuation of a larger narrative that spans across multiple lifetimes. The experiences, lessons, and talents we have accumulated over countless lifetimes are imprinted on our soul, shaping our desires, motivations, and potential in the present. By delving into these past lives, we can gain valuable insights into our soul's journey, recognizing the recurring themes, patterns, and gifts that have been woven into the fabric of our being.

One of the most powerful ways in which past life regression can help us step into our full potential is by revealing our past life passions and talents. We may discover that we were artists, healers, teachers, or warriors in previous incarnations, carrying those skills and inclinations into our present lives. By recognizing and embracing these innate gifts, we can unlock our full potential and find fulfillment in activities that resonate with our soul's deepest desires.

Past life regression can also help us to understand the karmic lessons we are here to learn. Karma, the law of cause and effect, suggests that our actions in past lives create energetic debts or imbalances that carry over into our present incarnation. By revisiting past lives, we can gain insight into these karmic patterns, recognizing the challenges we have chosen to overcome and the lessons we need to learn in this lifetime. This understanding can empower us to embrace our challenges with greater purpose and clarity, recognizing them as opportunities for growth and transformation.

Another way in which past life regression can empower us to step into our full potential is by revealing our soul contracts or agreements. These are agreements that we make with other souls before incarnating, outlining the lessons we wish to learn, the experiences we wish to have, and the relationships we wish to form. Sometimes, these soul contracts can involve challenging experiences or obstacles that are designed to help us grow and evolve. By understanding the purpose of these challenges, we can approach them with greater courage and determination, recognizing them as stepping stones on our path to fulfilling our potential.

Past life regression can also help us to connect with our spirit guides and higher selves. These wise and benevolent beings offer guidance and support throughout our soul's journey. By accessing past life experiences, we can often identify the spirit guides who have been with us throughout our many lifetimes. We may recognize familiar faces, hear comforting voices, or feel a sense of warmth and love surrounding us. This connection can provide us with a sense of comfort and reassurance, knowing that we are not alone on our journey and that we have the support of the spiritual realm.

Through past life regression, we can also develop a deeper understanding of our own soul's essence. By revisiting past lives, we can witness the evolution of our soul across time, recognizing the recurring themes, patterns, and lessons that have shaped our journey. This understanding can help us to connect with our deepest values, beliefs, and aspirations, aligning our lives with our soul's true purpose.

It is important to note that stepping into our full potential and living a life of purpose is not an overnight process. It requires a willingness to confront our shadows, to let go of limiting beliefs, and to embrace the unknown. It also involves taking action and making choices that are aligned with our newfound understanding of our soul's purpose. This may involve changing careers, ending toxic relationships, or pursuing new passions. However, the rewards are immeasurable. By living a life of purpose, we can experience a profound sense of fulfillment, joy, and meaning.

In conclusion, past life regression offers a powerful tool for stepping into our full potential and living a life of purpose. By exploring our past lives, we can gain valuable insights into our soul's journey, recognizing the recurring themes, patterns, and gifts that have shaped our being. We can uncover our hidden talents, understand our karmic lessons, and connect with our spirit guides and higher selves. This journey of self-discovery and empowerment can lead us to a more authentic, fulfilling, and joyful life, aligned with our soul's deepest desires.

ϸϸϸ

Our soul's journey is a river, flowing through time and carrying us towards our destiny. Through past life regression, we can navigate this river with greater awareness and intention, allowing us to reach our destination with grace and ease.

EIGHTEEN

JOURNEY THROUGH TIME TO UNCOVER YOUR SOUL'S HISTORY.

Life is an intricate tapestry woven with threads of experiences, emotions, and encounters that shape our present reality. Yet, the tapestry extends beyond the confines of a single lifetime, reaching back into the depths of time to encompass a multitude of past lives. Each life, a chapter in the grand saga of our soul's journey, holds valuable lessons, insights, and unresolved emotions that continue to influence our present existence. Past life regression offers a unique and transformative tool to embark on a journey through time, uncovering the hidden layers of our soul's history and gaining profound understanding of who we truly are.

The concept of reincarnation, central to past life regression, posits that our souls embark on multiple lifetimes, each one offering unique opportunities for growth, learning, and evolution. Through the process of reincarnation, we accumulate a wealth of experiences, knowledge, and wisdom that transcend the boundaries of a single lifetime. By accessing these past lives, we can tap into this vast reservoir of information, gaining valuable insights into our own patterns, behaviors, and tendencies.

Past life regression, through hypnosis or guided meditation, allows us to delve into the depths of our subconscious mind, where memories of past lives are stored. We can revisit these past lives, experiencing them as if we were living them in the present moment. These experiences can be incredibly vivid and emotional, offering a unique perspective on our current challenges, relationships, and life choices.

By journeying through time to uncover our soul's history, we can gain a deeper understanding of the root causes of our current struggles and challenges. We may discover unresolved traumas, emotional wounds, or karmic patterns that have been carried over from previous lifetimes. This understanding can empower us to heal old wounds, release emotional baggage, and break free from self-limiting beliefs.

Past life regression can also help us to understand the purpose and meaning of our current life. By exploring our past lives, we may discover recurring themes or patterns that indicate our soul's mission or purpose. We may also uncover hidden talents, skills, or passions that have been carried over from previous incarnations. This knowledge can guide us in making choices that are aligned with our soul's true calling, leading to a more fulfilling and purposeful life.

Through past life regression, we can also connect with loved ones who have passed on. By revisiting past lives where we shared deep bonds with these individuals, we can gain closure, heal old wounds, and find peace in our grief. We may also receive messages of love, guidance, or support, helping us to navigate our current challenges and find comfort in knowing that our loved ones are still with us in spirit.

Past life regression can also facilitate a deeper connection with our spirit guides and higher selves. These wise and benevolent beings offer guidance, support, and protection throughout our soul's journey. By accessing past life experiences, we can often identify the spirit guides who have been with us throughout our many lifetimes. This connection can provide us with a sense of comfort, reassurance, and direction, helping us to navigate our current challenges and make choices that are aligned with our highest good.

While the benefits of past life regression are numerous, it is important to approach this practice with an open mind and a healthy dose of skepticism. Not all experiences may be accurate or meaningful, and it is important to trust your own intuition and discernment when interpreting the information that emerges. It is also crucial to work with a qualified and experienced practitioner who can guide you through the process safely and effectively.

In conclusion, journeying through time to uncover your soul's history through past life regression is a transformative experience that can lead to profound healing, understanding, and growth. By exploring our past lives, we can gain valuable insights into our own patterns, behaviors, and tendencies. We can heal old wounds, release emotional baggage, understand our soul's purpose, connect with loved ones who have passed on, and deepen our relationship with our spirit guides. This journey of self-discovery can empower us to live a more conscious, intentional, and fulfilling life, aligned with our soul's true calling.

ﻆﻆﻆ

The past is not a burden, but a gift that offers us the opportunity to heal, grow, and transform. By embracing the wisdom of our past lives, we can unlock the door to our full potential and create a life of purpose, meaning, and joy.

NINETEEN

EMBARK ON A PATH OF SELF-DISCOVERY AND HEALING.

Life is an ever-unfolding journey of self-discovery, a continuous exploration of who we are, where we come from, and where we are going. We navigate through a labyrinth of experiences, emotions, and encounters, each one shaping our understanding of ourselves and the world around us. Yet, often we find ourselves lost, disconnected, and unsure of our path. Past life regression offers a transformative tool for embarking on a journey of self-discovery and healing, unveiling the hidden truths that lie dormant within us.

At its core, past life regression operates on the premise that our current life is not an isolated incident but rather a continuation of a larger narrative that spans across multiple lifetimes. The experiences, lessons, and traumas we have accumulated over countless lifetimes are imprinted on our soul, shaping our beliefs, values, and behaviors in the present. By delving into these past lives, we can gain valuable insights into our soul's journey, recognizing the recurring themes, patterns, and unresolved issues that may be influencing our current life path.

Past life regression, through hypnosis or guided meditation, allows us to access the vast reservoir of memories and emotions that lie dormant within our subconscious mind. We can revisit these past lives, experiencing them as if we were living them in the present moment. These experiences can be incredibly vivid and emotional, offering a unique perspective on our current challenges, relationships, and life choices.

By embarking on a journey through time, we can uncover hidden aspects of ourselves that we may not have been aware of. We may discover hidden talents, skills, or passions that have been carried over from previous incarnations. We may also gain a deeper understanding of our strengths, weaknesses, and vulnerabilities, allowing us to embrace our true selves with greater compassion and acceptance.

Past life regression can also help us to understand the root causes of our current challenges and struggles. We may discover unresolved traumas, emotional wounds, or karmic patterns that have been carried over from previous lifetimes. This understanding can empower us to heal old wounds, release emotional baggage, and break free from self-limiting beliefs. By addressing the underlying causes of our challenges, we can create lasting change and move forward on our journey of self-discovery with greater clarity and purpose.

Through past life regression, we can also connect with our spirit guides and higher selves. These wise and benevolent beings offer guidance, support, and protection throughout our soul's journey. By accessing past life experiences, we can often identify the spirit guides who have been with us throughout our many lifetimes. This connection can provide us with a sense of comfort, reassurance, and direction, helping us to navigate our current challenges and make choices that are aligned with our highest good.

Past life regression can also facilitate a deeper connection with our own intuition and inner wisdom. By revisiting past lives where we made choices that led to positive outcomes, we can strengthen our trust in our own inner guidance. This can empower us to make decisions that are aligned with our true desires and values, even when faced with uncertainty or external pressures.

The journey of self-discovery through past life regression is not always easy. It requires a willingness to confront our shadows, to acknowledge our own vulnerabilities, and to embrace the unknown. It can also be an emotional journey, as we revisit past traumas and unresolved conflicts. However, the rewards are immeasurable. By delving into our past lives, we can gain a deeper understanding of who we are, where we come from, and where we are going. We can heal old wounds, release emotional baggage, and connect with our soul's true purpose. This newfound awareness can empower us to live a more authentic, joyful, and fulfilling life, aligned with our highest potential.

In conclusion, embarking on a path of self-discovery and healing through past life regression is a transformative experience that can lead to profound growth, understanding, and empowerment. By exploring our past lives, we can gain valuable insights into our own patterns, behaviors, and tendencies. We can heal old wounds, release emotional baggage, and connect with our soul's true purpose. This journey of self-discovery can empower us to live a more conscious, intentional, and fulfilling life, aligned with our highest good.

ϷϷϷ

Our soul's journey is a symphony of interconnected lives, each one playing a unique role in the grand orchestration of our existence. Through past life regression, we can hear the music of our soul, allowing us to dance to the rhythm of our own unique song.

TWENTY

UNLEASH THE POWER OF PAST LIFE REGRESSION FOR LASTING CHANGE.

In the tapestry of our lives, the threads of our past, present, and future are intricately interwoven. The choices we make, the experiences we have, and the lessons we learn shape our understanding of ourselves and the world around us. Yet, often we find ourselves trapped in repetitive patterns, plagued by unresolved emotions, and unsure of our true purpose. Past life regression offers a powerful tool to unravel the mysteries of our past, unleash our hidden potential, and create lasting change in our lives.

At its core, past life regression operates on the premise that our current life is not an isolated incident but rather a continuation of a larger narrative that spans across multiple lifetimes. The unresolved traumas, emotional wounds, and negative experiences we carry from past lives can significantly impact our present well-being, manifesting as physical ailments, emotional challenges, or self-limiting beliefs. By delving into these past experiences, we can gain valuable insights into the root causes of our current struggles, allowing us to address and heal the underlying wounds.

Past life regression, through hypnosis or guided meditation, allows us to access the vast reservoir of memories and emotions that lie dormant within our subconscious mind. We can revisit these past lives, experiencing them as if we were living them in the present moment. These experiences can be incredibly vivid and emotional, offering a unique perspective on our current challenges, relationships, and life choices.

By unleashing the power of past life regression, we can initiate a profound transformation in our lives. One of the most significant ways in which past life regression can create lasting change is by releasing trapped emotions. When we experience traumatic events, the associated emotions can become trapped in our energy field, creating blockages that manifest as physical or emotional ailments. By revisiting these past experiences, we can allow these emotions to surface and be processed, releasing the energetic hold they have on us. This emotional release can lead to a profound sense of relief and liberation, freeing us from the weight of past traumas and opening up space for healing and growth.

Past life regression can also help us to identify and reframe negative beliefs and thought patterns that may be contributing to our current challenges. Often, we hold onto limiting beliefs about ourselves, others, or the world around us, based on past experiences or societal conditioning. These beliefs can create self-fulfilling prophecies, attracting experiences that reinforce our negative self-perceptions. By exploring the origins of these beliefs in past lives, we can challenge their validity and replace them with more positive and empowering thoughts. This shift in perspective can profoundly impact our present lives, opening us up to new possibilities and opportunities.

Another way in which past life regression can create lasting change is by resolving past life conflicts and relationships. We may discover that we have unresolved conflicts or karmic debts with individuals in our current lives that stem from past life interactions. By revisiting these past life experiences, we can gain a deeper understanding of the dynamics of these relationships and find ways to heal and resolve them in the present. This can lead to deeper, more meaningful connections with others, fostering a sense of forgiveness, compassion, and understanding.

Past life regression can also help us to discover our soul's purpose and passion. Often, we feel lost or unfulfilled in our lives, unsure of our direction or purpose. By exploring past lives, we may discover recurring themes, passions, or talents that have carried over from lifetime to lifetime. This can provide us with valuable clues about our true calling, inspiring us to pursue activities that align with our soul's deepest desires.

Through past life regression, we can also connect with our spirit guides and higher selves, gaining access to a wellspring of wisdom and guidance that can help us to navigate our current challenges and make choices that are aligned with our highest good. This connection can provide us with a sense of peace, acceptance, and understanding, even in the face of adversity.

It is important to note that unleashing the power of past life regression for lasting change is not a passive process. It requires a willingness to confront our shadows, to explore our past with an open heart and mind, and to actively integrate the lessons and insights we gain into our present lives. It also involves taking action and making choices that are aligned with our newfound understanding of ourselves and our purpose.

In conclusion, past life regression is a powerful tool for unleashing our hidden potential and creating lasting change in our lives. By exploring our past lives, we can heal old wounds, release emotional baggage, reframe limiting beliefs, resolve past life conflicts, discover our soul's purpose, and connect with our inner wisdom. This journey of self-discovery and healing can empower us to live a more authentic, joyful, and purposeful life, where we are free to embrace our true selves and create the reality we desire.

ϷϷϷ

The past is not a distant memory, but a living presence within us. By embracing the wisdom of our past lives, we can unlock the door to our true potential and create a life that is aligned with our soul's deepest desires.

TWENTY-ONE
SUMMARY

Echoes of the Past: Healing Through Past Life Regression - A Summary

The journey of self-discovery is a profound and transformative experience that can lead us to a deeper understanding of ourselves, our purpose, and our place in the world. Past life regression offers a unique and powerful tool for embarking on this journey, allowing us to explore the hidden depths of our soul's history and unlock our full potential.

Through the lens of past life regression, we recognize that our current lives are not isolated incidents but rather continuations of a larger narrative that spans across multiple lifetimes. The experiences, lessons, and traumas we have accumulated over countless lifetimes are imprinted on our soul, shaping our beliefs, values, and behaviors in the present. By accessing these past lives, we can gain valuable insights into the recurring themes, patterns, and unresolved issues that may be influencing our current life path.

By unlocking the secrets of our soul's journey, we can uncover hidden aspects of ourselves that we may not have been aware of. We may discover hidden talents, skills, or passions that have been carried over from previous incarnations. We can also heal old wounds, release emotional baggage, and break free from self-limiting beliefs that have been holding us back.

One of the most profound benefits of past life regression is the ability to identify and heal old wounds and traumas. By revisiting past experiences, we can gain a deeper understanding of the root causes of our current emotional and physical struggles. We may discover unresolved conflicts, unprocessed grief, or deeply ingrained patterns of self-sabotage that have been carried over from previous lifetimes. By facing these issues head-on, we can release pent-up emotions, forgive ourselves and others, and ultimately break free from the cycle of pain and suffering.

Past life regression can also help us to gain a greater understanding of our relationships with others. We may discover karmic connections with loved ones, soulmates, or even adversaries, shedding light on the dynamics of our current interactions. By recognizing the karmic patterns that play out in our relationships, we can learn valuable lessons about forgiveness, compassion, and unconditional love.

Another significant benefit of past life regression is the opportunity to reconnect with our soul's purpose and potential. By exploring our past lives, we may discover hidden talents, skills, or passions that have been carried over from previous incarnations. We may also gain a clearer understanding of our life's mission and the unique gifts we have to offer the world. This newfound clarity can empower us to make bold choices, pursue our dreams, and live a more authentic and fulfilling life.

Through past life regression, we can also experience profound healing and transformation. By releasing trapped emotions, healing past traumas, and reframing negative beliefs, we can create lasting change in our lives. We can break free from self-sabotaging patterns, cultivate inner peace and self-love, and step into our full potential.

By journeying through time to uncover our soul's history, we can gain valuable insights into our own patterns, behaviors, and tendencies. We can heal old wounds, release emotional baggage, understand our soul's purpose, connect with loved ones who have passed on, and deepen our relationship with our spirit guides. This newfound awareness can empower us to live a more conscious, intentional, and fulfilling life, aligned with our highest good.

Embarking on a path of self-discovery and healing through past life regression is a transformative experience that can lead to profound growth, understanding, and empowerment. By exploring our past lives, we can gain valuable insights into our own patterns, behaviors, and tendencies. We can heal old wounds, release emotional baggage, understand our soul's purpose, connect with loved ones who have passed on, and deepen our relationship with our spirit guides. This journey of self-discovery can empower us to live a more conscious, intentional, and fulfilling life, aligned with our highest good.

By unleashing the power of past life regression, we can create lasting change in our lives. We can break free from self-limiting beliefs, heal old wounds, and reconnect with our soul's purpose. This journey of self-discovery and healing can empower us to live a more authentic, joyful, and fulfilling life, aligned with our highest potential.

ᐅᐅᐅ

Citation And References

This book represents the culmination of extensive research and meticulous analysis, incorporating a diverse range of sources, including numerous books, scholarly studies, and personal experiences. Additionally, I have scoured various websites to gather relevant information and data essential for the compilation of this work. I have taken every precaution to ensure the accuracy of the information presented and have diligently cited all sources to acknowledge their contributions.

Despite these efforts, the possibility of inadvertent errors remains. I deeply value the insights of my readers and appreciate any feedback that can help identify and rectify such inaccuracies. I encourage you to bring any discrepancies to my attention.

Your feedback is not only welcome but crucial, as it will aid in correcting current editions and enhancing the content of future ones. I am committed to maintaining the highest standards of accuracy and reliability in my work and thank you for your support and understanding.

Additionally, I firmly uphold the principle of freedom of speech and expression as guaranteed under Article 19(1)(a) of the Constitution of India, and I respect the diverse viewpoints and expressions of all readers.

ppp

Other Books Of The Author

1. Empowering Minds: A Journey into Women's Self-Discovery and Power
2. The Dynamics of Motivation: Catalyzing Thought into Action
3. Meditation and Mental Well Being: The Path to Inner Peace and Clarity
4. The Psychology of Child Education: Nurturing Future Generations
5. Ethical Enlightenment: A Modern Guide to Living with Integrity
6. Voices of Empowerment: Stories of Women Rising Against Odds
7. Social Psychology in Everyday Life: Understanding Human Connections
8. The Essence of Motivational Speaking: Inspiring Change in Others
9. Balancing Acts: Women, Work, and the Will to Lead
10. Guiding with Grace: Raising Children with Compassion and Awareness
11. The Power of Positive Aging: Embracing Life After Fifty
12. Building Resilient Communities: Social Work in Action
13. The Ethical Educator: Principles for Teaching and Learning
14. From Insight to Impact: Social Psychology for a Better World
15. The Ethics of Empathy: A Guide to Ethical Living
16. The Science of Empowering the Self: Navigating Life's Challenges with Psychological Wisdom
17. The Mindful Conscious Leader: Meditation Techniques for Modern Management
18. Pioneering Spirit: Women's Pathways to Leadership and Empowerment
19. Feeling to Healing: The Role of Emotional Intelligence in Child Development
20. Transformative Talks and Words of Inspiration: Insights into Motivational Oratory

21. Green Ethics: A Path to Sustainable Living
22. Spiritual Integrity: Navigating Life with Moral Compassion
23. Clean Living, Clean Society: The Ethics of Cleanliness
24. Patriotic Spirits: Building a Nation on Positive Attitudes
25. Innovative Integrity & Vibrant Visions: The Ethical and Entrepreneurial Spirit of Gujarat
26. Youthful Visions, Endless Possibilities: Inspiring Ethics and Motivation in Children
27. Living Your Legacy: How to Motivate Others by Living Your Values
28. Secret of Healing Conversations: Ethical Practices in Counselling and Therapy
29. Creative Kindness: Crafting a Life of Compassion and Creativity
30. The Power of Appreciation: How Gratitude Can Transform Your Relationships
31. Bhagavad-Gita: Messages
32. Science of Art: The New Frontier of Fashion Modernism
33. Vivekananda's Virtues: A Blueprint for Modern Living
34. Empower Her: Navigating the Path to Women's Entrepreneurship
35. The Boundless Classroom: Innovations in Global Education
36. The Language of Leadership: Communicating with Authenticity and Impact
37. The Warrior's Mantra: Deciphering the Hanuman Chalisa
38. Echoes of Empathy: Transformative Stories of Social Service
39. Artful Living: Cultivating Creativity in Your Daily Routine
40. Finding Your Why: Discovering Your Passions and Charting Your Course
41. The Role of Social Media in Shaping Self-Esteem and Interpersonal Relationships among Adolescents
42. Karma's Tapestry: Weaving a Life of Selfless Service
43. Altruistic Alchemy: Transforming Lives Through Giving
44. The Blueprint of Pro-Activeness and Productivity: Crafting Habits for Success
45. The Simplicity with Grounded Wisdom: Embracing Authenticity

in a Complex World

46. Secret of Solopreneur's Odyssey: Navigating the Path to Self-Employment
47. Exploring Tapestry of Peace: Global Perspectives on Harmony
48. The Art and Actions of Connection: Mastering Communication for Impact
49. She Governs and at the Helm: Strategies for Political Empowerment
50. Rising Above and Rising with Grace: A Woman's Roadmap to Career Mastery
51. The Effect of Networking & Connectedness: Building Strategic Alliances for Women
52. Beyond his Barriers: Women Thriving in Male-Dominated Fields
53. Secret of Inner Compass: Navigating Life with Intuition
54. Creative & Pro-Active Muses: A Celebration of Women in the Arts
55. Unburdened: The Art of Releasing the Past
56. Amplified Voices: Speeches of Women that Astonished the World
57. Secret of Manifesting Dreams: A Woman's Guide to Intentional Living
58. Ethics and Value Based Education: Reimagining Japan's School System
59. The Moral Compass Curriculum: A Holistic Approach
60. Tech with Heart: Integrating Ethics into Digital Learning
61. Honoring Virtue: Recognizing Ethical Excellence in Education
62. Raising Good Humans: A Guide to Character Development
63. The Spark Within: Nurturing Creativity in Children
64. The Teenager Whisperer: Navigating Adolescence with Grace
65. Igniting a Passion for Learning: Inspiring Lifelong Curiosity
66. The Habit Lab: Cultivating Positive Behaviors in Children
67. Seeds of Empathy: Fostering Compassion in Young Hearts
68. The Reading Revolution: Inspiring a Love of Books in Children
69. The Learning Brain: Unlocking the Secrets of Student Success
70. Teaching for All: Differentiated Instruction Strategies
71. The Time Alchemist: Mastering Time Management for Peak Performance

72. The Resilience Factor: Transforming Setbacks into Stepping Stones
73. The Healing Touch of Nature: An Introduction to Naturopathy
74. Echoes of the Past: Healing Through Past Life Regression
75. The Spiritual Healer's Handbook: Exploring Energy Medicine
76. Crystal Clarity: Unveiling the Power of Gemstones
77. The Dream Weaver's Guide: Decoding the Language of Dreams
78. Emotional Alchemy: Transforming Pain into Power
79. Sonic Serenity: Harnessing Sound for Stress Relief
80. The Entrepreneur's Playbook: Launching Your Business with Confidence
81. Productivity Unleashed: Time Management Strategies for Entrepreneurs
82. The Problem Solver's Toolkit: Creative Solutions for Business Challenges
83. The Future is Now: Emerging Trends in Business
84. The Curious Explorer: A Child's Guide to Scientific Discovery
85. Digital Pioneers: Empowering Kids in the Tech World
86. The Young Philosopher's Guide: Exploring Life's Big Questions
87. Finding Your Voice: Communication Skills for Confident Kids
88. Nature's Playground: A Child's Guide to Outdoor Adventure
89. Growing a Greener Tomorrow: A Guide to Tree Planting & Conservation
90. Driving with Purpose: Ethical Choices on the Road
91. The Healing Touch: Cultivating Compassion in Healthcare
92. Navigating the Digital Landscape: Ethics in the Age of Social Media
93. The Ethical Closet: A Guide to Sustainable Fashion
94. The Mindful Voyager: Sustainable Travel Practices
95. The Feminine Divine: Honoring the Goddesses of India
96. Sacred Sounds: Chanting Your Way to Inner Peace
97. The Yoga Path: Uniting with the Divine Within
98. Rites of Passage: Creating Meaningful Ceremonies
99. The Chakra System: A Map of Inner Transformation
100. Spiritual Sangha: Finding Community through Satsang and

Bhajan

101. Pilgrimage of the Soul: Spiritual Journeys in India

ϸϸϸ

Contact

Dr. Minakshi Bansal
Social Activist
Ahmedabad, Gujarat, Bharat
minakshiindiag20@yahoo.com

❦❦❦

|| LOKAHA SAMASTHAHA SUKHINO BHAVANTU ||